CONTENTS

A NOTE TO THE READER

A Collage of Crafts is a book of projects, but it can also be used as a book of ideas. Readers can adapt the techniques and materials described and invent their own craft projects.

Here are some things to keep in mind when using this book:

• Some of the projects require the use of an X-acto knife. These are extremely sharp (much sharper than most kitchen knives) and should be used carefully. Anyone who is using an X-acto knife for the first time should ask an adult for help.

• When cutting anything with a knife, always put a wooden board or thick cardboard underneath. This protects the work surface, and also provides a smooth cutting surface.

• Whenever a project requires paint, glue, or plaster, cover the work surface with newspaper before starting.

• When using a strong glue (such as Super Glue or clear glue), squeeze it directly from the tube. Wipe off any excess glue with a cloth. A drop or two is enough for most projects.

CARDBOARD DRAWERS

Equipment
- cardboard box with drawers
- old newspapers
- 2 brushes (small and medium)
- pencil
- square rule
- paste
- glue roller
- scissors

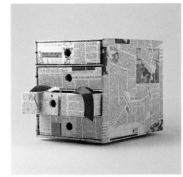

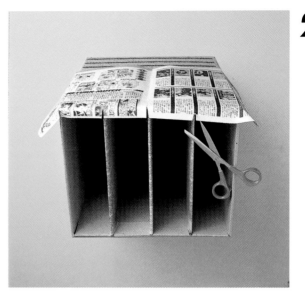

Cover the sides of the box. Place a large piece of newspaper on the top and cut it to size. Make small notches in the paper to fit it around the sides of the shelves. Spread paste on the newspaper and attach to the box. Smooth paper.

Start by covering the edges of the horizontal supports between the cardboard drawers. Measure and cut a piece of newspaper to the width of each shelf. Cut the edges on an angle and fold them inside. Use the roller to spread the paste. Paste the paper onto the supports. Smooth down the newspaper to push out air bubbles.

To cover the front of the drawers, place a piece of newspaper over the front. If there is a hole, trace its shape with a pencil on the reverse side of the newspaper. Cut notches in the paper with the scissors. Spread paste on the newspaper and carefully place it over the hole. Fold the cut sections toward the inside.

4

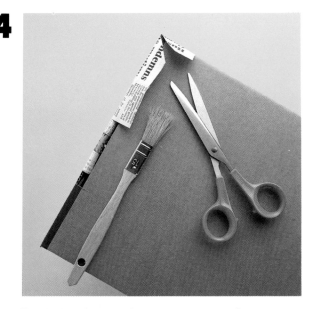

Finish the drawers by pasting strips of newspaper to the sides. To finish the corners, fold the strip of paper toward the underside of the drawer and cut it at an angle to fit. Paste in place.

5

When the set of drawers is finished, add small pieces of cut or torn newspaper to the outside, pasting them in various directions.

MAGAZINE RACK

Give a new look to a magazine rack by adding brightly colored comic strips. Tear, cut, and paste the pieces in a design or in a random pattern. (For the hole, see instructions for the drawers on page 9, step 3.)

FILE

Paste comic strips onto a cardboard file, extending them about 3/4 inch beyond the sides. Fold these edges inside and tape down securely. Tear small pieces of comic strips and paste them all over the file for decoration.

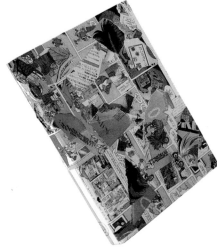

COMIC STRIP LAMP

Equipment

- folded paper lampshade
- comic strips
- cord or string
- punch, awl, or Phillips screwdriver
- hammer
- plastic folder blade or plastic ruler
- brush
- paste
- ruler

2 Reshape the lampshade and re-paste its edges. Let dry. Thread a colored cord (or string) through the holes at the top and tie in a bow. Make a knot at each end of the cord. Place the shade back on the lamp.

1 Open the lampshade and lay it flat. Brush paste on a comic strip (or on several small pieces) and attach to the shade. Place it under weights to dry (heavy books work well). When it is completely dry, find the holes on the underside of the shade. Use the punch and hammer (place a board underneath) to make new holes. Use the ruler and folder blade to repleat the lamp shade along its original folds.

FRAME

Tear or cut pieces of newspaper and paste them to a picture frame, making sure to overlap the pieces. Decorate the mat board in the same way. Paste a photograph or other picture to the mat board. Attach a self-adhesive picture hanger on the back.

SEWING MACHINE

Create an unusual sculpture by covering a broken sewing machine (or other small appliance) with torn newspapers or comic strips. Don't forget to add the spool of thread as a final touch!

This technique can also be used to cover old toys.

12

PAPER GETS ITS NAME FROM A PLANT: PAPYRUS

Long before paper was invented, the Egyptians learned to make the papyrus plant into paperlike sheets. Over four thousand years ago, the Egyptians cut the plant into long, thin slices, moistened the pieces, and laid them next to each other on a board. Then they placed other pieces on top, at right angles to the first layer. Next, the two layers were pressed together and beaten with a hammer. The plant's sap glued the slices together as they dried, making them into a light brown sheet, which

was then polished and smoothed with stones or shells. Sometimes the sheets would be made into long scrolls. The longest known scroll is 133 feet long. Papyrus fibers are very strong—so strong that they were made not only into sheets but into shoes, sails, ropes, baskets, and even small boats.

THE INVENTION OF PAPER

Paper is believed to have been invented in A.D. 105 by a Chinese court official named Ts'ai Lun. Ts'ai Lun made his paper from bark, hemp, rags, and old fish nets. These were pounded into a pulp and mixed with water. A screen made of bamboo strips was then dipped into the wet pulp. As the water drained away, the thin layer of pulp dried into a sheet of paper.

The Chinese kept the secret of papermaking for five hundred years. Then the craft of papermaking spread to Japan, and later to the Middle East and Europe. The development of printing in Europe (in the middle of the fifteenth century) created a huge demand for paper.

EARLY WRITING MATERIALS

Even before the Egyptians wrote on papyrus, ancient cultures made things to write on. Six thousand years ago, the Sumerians, who lived in the Middle East, wrote on clay tablets. The Greeks and Romans covered wooden boards with wax or plaster and cut letters into them with tools made of bone or metal. These boards could be tied together with thongs to make books—very heavy books!

For thousands of years after their invention, papyrus sheets were the most common writing "paper." Then, around A.D. 200–300, parchment became more popular because it was less expensive than papyrus. Parchment was made from animal skins, usually from the skin of sheep, goats, or calves. The hair was scraped from the skin, then the skin was scraped, polished, stretched, and rubbed with chalk or pumice.

THE BIRTH OF AN ART FORM: COLLAGE

Collages are artworks made by gluing pieces of paper, cardboard, cloth, newspaper, photographs, or other objects to a flat surface. Sometimes the artist draws a picture on top of the pasted materials. The word collage comes from the French word coller, which means "to paste." Collages are so common now that children in nursery school make them, but they were a revolutionary art form when the artists Pablo Picasso and Georges Braque began making them, around 1912–1913. During that era, shortly before World War I, many artists were rebelling against old traditions of painting and sculpture. Picasso and Braque deliberately set out to create artworks of ordinary materials. Their collages shocked people at that time but are now recognized as important works of art.

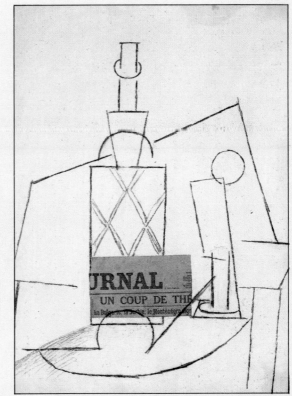

Pablo Picasso. *Bottle and Glass*. 1912

Georges Braque. *Violin and Pipe*. 1913–14.

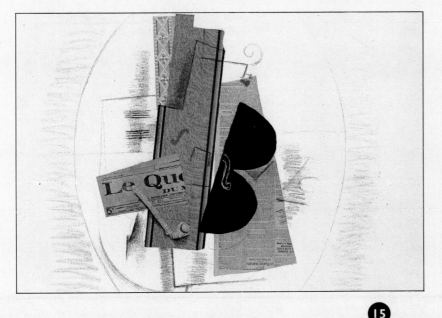

PAPERMAKING

Until the middle of the nineteenth century, most paper was made from rags by means of the process invented by the Chinese. That method was slow, and it had another limitation: paper manufacturers couldn't get enough rags. During the nineteenth century, people learned to make paper from wood pulp, and developed machines to speed up the papermaking process. Today, paper is made from rags, wood, and many other substances.

NATURE COLLAGE

Equipment
- plants of all kinds: leaves, wheat, twigs, bark, moss, chestnuts, dried flowers.
- a wooden crate or 1 furring strip
- cardboard (3 x 3 feet)
- paint brush
- blue and white poster paints
- pencil
- wood glue
- glue roller (or a piece of cardboard to spread glue)
- clear glue
- glue brush
- ruler
- pruning shears
- scissors
- clips

1

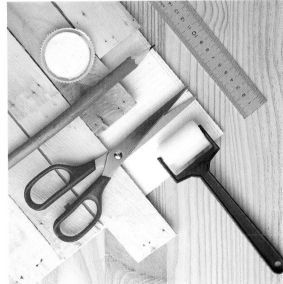

Find a wooden crate and take it apart to get 5 slats of equal length or cut furring strips. Measure them, and then transfer their dimensions to the

piece of cardboard. Cut the cardboard and cover it with wood glue. Attach the slats to the cardboard one by one. Put a weight on the slats and let dry.

2

While the glue is drying, use the shears to cut 4 small branches for the frame. If desired, sharpen the ends using the shears (or an X-acto knife). Glue them around the edges with wood glue, holding them in place with clips until dry.

The design shown in the photographs is just a suggestion.

3

Draw a picture on the wood in pencil, pressing hard to mark the lines clearly.

4

Use the blue and white paints to color in the sky and clouds.

5

Cut small twigs with the shears or knife to form the house. Use wood glue to glue them next to each other lengthwise. Make a path with small round sections of wood. Use moss, leaves, and dried flowers to make the garden. Make a fence from extra pieces of wood. If necessary, repaint the sky.

6

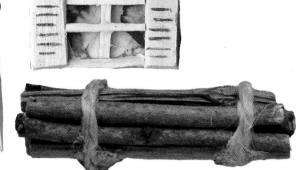

Use wood from the crate to make a door for the house and cut a tiny, round twig for a door handle. Use the shears or knife to cut small pieces of wood for the window. Dried flower petals can be glued to a piece of paper to make the curtains. Tie a bundle of twigs to make firewood.

7 Finish the scene by adding a field of wheat, a few ivy leaves for shrubs, and chestnuts as rocks. Attach the bundle of firewood. Large leaves can be used as trees. Work slowly and carefully, gluing one plant onto picture at a time. Attach 2 self-adhesive picture hangers on the back and hang the scene on a wall.

NATURE POTS

Equipment

- twigs
- empty cans and flower pots
- florist's moss
- thin rope
- twine
- green paint
- glue brush
- small paint brush
- clear glue
- shears

A few cut laurel leaves, glued down and then varnished, give this small clay pot a new look. Be sure to overlap the leaves.

Paint the edges of an empty can. Let it dry thoroughly. Coat the can with glue and wrap the rope all around it. Moss (or small twigs cut to the dimension of the can) can also be used as coverings.

Cover a rectangular clay pot with pieces of bark. A drop of glue on each piece will be enough.

FLOWER PRESS

Equipment

- cardboard
- 2 sheets of drawing paper (different colors)
- leaves and flowers
- 4 bolts with wing nuts
- hammer
- punch, awl, or Phillips screwdriver
- varnish
- small brush
- pencil
- paste or white glue
- X-acto knife
- scissors
- ruler

cardboard, as shown. Mark the cardboard carefully so that the holes line up. Flowers and leaves can be pressed and dried between any of the layers.

Pressed flowers and leaves can be used in numerous craft projects.

To decorate the flower press, cut a 7-inch square out of one of the colored sheets of paper and cut off its corners. Glue it to one of the pieces of cardboard and let it dry with a weight on it. When it is completely dry, punch 4 holes through the colored square. (These must match the holes in the other pieces of cardboard.) Measure and cut out a smaller square from the other colored paper and glue laurel leaves on it. Carefully varnish the leaves. Glue this to the colored piece of cardboard. Hold the pieces of cardboard together, leaving the decorated piece on the top. Slide the bolts through each hole from underneath and screw on the wing nuts.

Measure and cut out six 7-inch squares of cardboard. Cut off the corners of each at an angle. Punch out 4 holes in the corners of each piece of

Throughout history, people have been fascinated with plants and have attributed various powers and virtues to them.

BOTANY, AN ANCIENT STORY

The earliest known essay about plants is forty centuries old. It was written by the Chinese scholar Li Che Teng, who described more than one thousand plants. In the year 1000 B.C., a similar work was written in India. The Roman authors Cato and Pliny the Elder wrote works on the virtues of

Fourteenth century Latin manuscript based on an earlier Greek manuscript by Dioscorides.

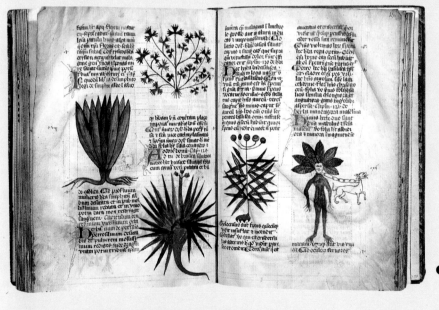

plants. In the Middle Ages, Paracelsus, a Swiss doctor, believed that "the pastures and hills are potential pharmacies." Most of the earliest writings about plants were herbals, manuals that identified plants so that they could be used as medicines.

PORTRAIT OF A FAMOUS NATURE LOVER

The French writer and philosopher Jean-Jacques Rousseau (1712–1778) loved nature and read all the existing literature on the subject. During a trip to Switzerland, he made friends with Doctor Jean-Antoine d'Ivernois, a naturalist and doctor. They exchanged letters in which they compared views about botany. Rousseau often gathered plants during his walks. The study of botany allowed him to combine his hunger for knowledge with the pleasure of long contemplative walks.

The Greek physician and pharmacologist Pedanius Dioscorides (A.D. 40?–90?) wrote an herbal that remained important for sixteen centuries. Dioscorides's herbal identified about six hundred plants and the drugs that could be made from them. Most of the drugs he described remained in use until modern times.

THE LANGUAGE OF FLOWERS

Flowers have often been believed to speak a language of their own. Each flower means something different, although the meanings vary depending on the civilization and the century. For instance, in the Middle Ages, the rose had a religious meaning and a secular (nonreligious) meaning. In religious art, it symbolized the Virgin Mary, while in secular art it symbolized romantic love.

In China, the tree peony symbolized good fortune. Plants besides flowers had meanings, too. An arrangement of pine, bamboo, and a particular long-lived fungus meant "long life."

In Japan, cherry blossoms symbolized the samurai, the professional warriors, because cherry blossoms are beautiful, bloom early, and die soon after blooming.

During the nineteenth century, several popular books were written about the language of flowers. Courting couples could send messages to each other using flowers instead of words.

THE MANDRAKE

No plant is so steeped in superstition as the mandrake, whose forked root looks like the human body. Although in the Middle Ages witches were accused of using the root for evil purposes, it was also believed to make pregnancy easier, to help people sleep better, and even to help in obtaining love and riches. Releasing the powers of the plant wasn't easy, though. It had to be pulled from the ground at night, by the light of the moon, and certain prayers and rituals were necessary. Some people believed that a black dog must pull the root from the ground by a cord so that it was never touched by human hands.

The Language of Flowers,
French, about 1850.

THREE-DIMENSIONAL POSTCARDS

Equipment
- vacation photographs
- sheet of colored paper
- Bristol board
- sheet of flexible plastic
- small shells
- sand
- pencil
- clear glue
- double-sided tape
- scissors
- ruler

2

Cut the colored paper to the size of the photograph. Draw 3 horizontal lines for the address, a vertical line down the middle, and a square in the upper right-hand corner for the stamp. Decorate it with felt-tip pens if desired.

1

Measure the photograph with the ruler. Cut the Bristol board to the same size. Spread the glue on the back of the board and attach the photograph. Let it dry for 5 minutes.

TIP:

Miniature toys or pictures cut out from magazines can be added along with the sand and shells.

3

Cut a piece of plastic, making it 3/4 inch larger than the photograph. Place it on the photograph and fold 3 of the sides to the back. Hold them in place with the double-sided tape. Put in sand and shells through the open side, then close this last side with double-sided tape.

4 Glue the photograph to the back of the colored paper, pressing it down firmly.

TIP:
To keep the shells clean and bug-free, scrub them with a toothbrush dipped in water mixed with a few drops of dishwashing liquid. Rinse them well and let dry before gluing them to the bowl.

AQUARIUM

To make your goldfish feel like it's in the Caribbean, glue a row of pretty shells around its bowl. (Clear glue works well on glass.) To create an interesting effect, lean the bowl on a slope while adding layers of different colors of sand and pebbles. Everything will stay in place when the bowl is set upright again.

LAMP

Use an old wall light fixture with a wide rim. Start by gluing the small shells around the lamp, then attach the larger ones. Let it dry thoroughly before hanging it on the wall.

FRAME

Place a selection of small, medium, and large shells around an old frame. Always glue down the smallest shells first. Let the glue dry completely. Then make a cardboard mat board and paste a sheet of colored paper on it. Fasten a self-adhesive picture hanger on the back. This makes a great frame for a swimming certificate or beach photos.

Use this technique to decorate frames or lamps with many other small objects such as pebbles or stamps.

PAPER CLIP HOLDER

A large clam shell and a smaller one, glued together, make a great paper clip holder. Place a large drop of glue on the top of the small shell and put the large shell on top of it. Let it dry 30 minutes.

BOXES

A plain cardboard box becomes decorative when covered with shells. Glue the small shells with clear glue; make sure the glue is dry before continuing with the larger shells.

LETTER HOLDER

This is made from 4 scallop shells and a few smaller shells for support. Also glue the bottom scallop shell to a round shell. Use the clear glue generously to make a strong letter holder. Place supports around it and let it dry overnight.

TIP:

To make the shells look shiny, apply a single coat of varnish to the finished box.

There are many different ways to arrange the shells. One way is to sort the shells according to size and glue tiny ones all around the box and on part of the cover (see photograph on right). Then glue the medium and large shells on the top of the box.

Try painting the box before attaching the shells. Let the paint dry thoroughly before gluing them on.

A PASSION FOR COLLECTING

A collector is someone who enjoys gathering objects that share a common theme. Different theories have been suggested to explain this need to collect and the pleasure obtained from it, but no one fully understands it.

COLLECTORS' NAMES

The most common collections have given rise to names that designate the collector: philatelists collect stamps; numismatists, coins, paper money, and medals; philuminists, match boxes; and conchophiles, shells.

PHILATELY (STAMP COLLECTING)

The first postage stamps became available in 1840, in England, and stamps became collectors' items almost immediately. At first, philatelists would try to collect every kind of stamp, from all over the world, but as more and more stamps were issued, this became impossible. Soon collectors began to look for stamps from one country or from one time period. Later, collecting stamps by subject became popular. For instance, a person might collect stamps with pictures of birds or flags. Some collectors look for stamps with errors such as printing mistakes or perforation holes that run across the picture.

PEOPLE COLLECT

ALL SORTS OF THINGS

It would be impossible to make a complete list of the different collections that exist. Common ones include stamps, coins, baseball cards, model cars and trains, postcards, and images of a particular animal such as the cat or horse. People also collect salt shakers, lunch boxes, teddy bears, antique toys, license plates, thimbles, buttons, hubcaps, pens, rocks, stickers, bugs, and many, many other things. Some people see their collections as an investment and study the monetary value of each item; others simply enjoy owning and learning about the objects.

A DIFFERENT KIND OF COLLECTION

The purpose of some collections is not to gather objects of a particular type, but to obtain anything that concerns a specific person. Autograph hunters are one example of this kind of collector. There are also those who are willing to face bankruptcy to purchase anything that once belonged to their idol. When English pop star Elton John offered numerous personal belongings for sale, collectors were willing to pay huge amounts of money just to own things once owned by Elton John.

THE COLLECTOR'S FRENZY

Collectors are always on the lookout for the missing element in their collections; some are even willing to spend a fortune or travel enormous distances to add to their collections. Swatch watches, for example, have become so popular that some collectors fly to Switzerland every time a new watch comes out, just to have the latest design!

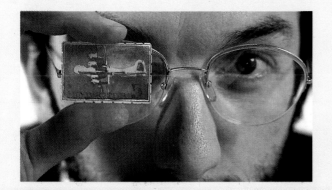

COLLECTOR'S SHOWCASE

Equipment
- cardboard box
- corrugated cardboard
- 2 self-adhesive picture hangers
- pencil
- paper tape
- paste
- small glue roller
- X-acto knife
- square rule

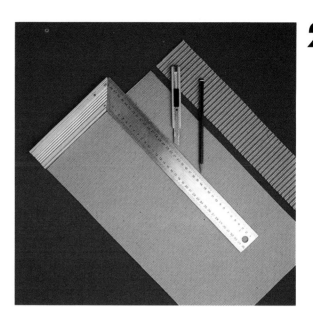

2

Measure and cut four 4-inch-wide strips to fit all around the inside edges of the box.

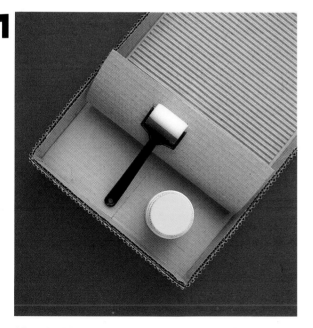

1

Use the X-acto knife to cut the sides of the box to 4 inches high. Measure the bottom of the box and cut a piece of corrugated cardboard to fit inside it. Roll paste on the back of the cardboard and paste it inside the box.

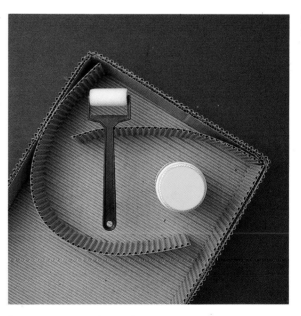

3

Paste strips in place, then measure, cut, and paste strips to fit around the outside of the box.

4

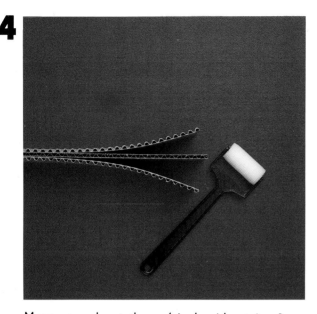

Measure and cut three 4-inch-wide strips from parts of the cardboard box that were cut off. Each must be the length of the inside of the showcase. Paste a strip of cardboard to each side to make the strips stronger.

NOTE:

Because the separations are not pasted in place, they can be moved around for different collections. The showcase is very strong.

6

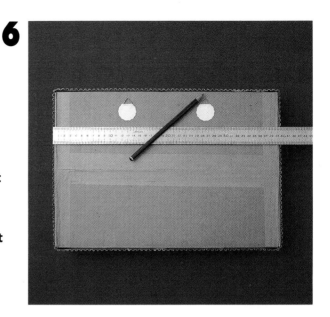

Turn the box over and attach the 2 picture hangers. Measure the distances carefully so that it hangs straight.

5

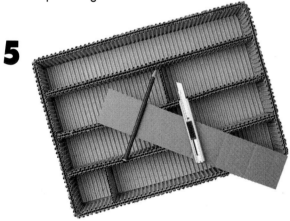

These strips don't have to be glued in place. They are held in place by the corrugations of the cardboard. Cut out small vertical separators from an extra piece of cardboard.

BLOTTER PAD

Equipment

- tagboard
- sheet of colored paper
- large piece of blotting paper
- kraft paper
- small piece of corrugated cardboard
- pencil
- paste
- X-acto knife
- scissors
- ruler

Measure, cut, and paste the colored paper to the tagboard. The paper should entirely cover it. Measure, cut, and fold pieces of kraft paper to make corners, as shown. Paste them onto the corners of tagboard, putting paste only on the back.

Measure and cut 4 corrugated cardboard triangles and paste them to the corners. Cut the blotting paper slightly smaller than the blotting pad to show the sheet of colored paper underneath. Slide the blotting paper under the corner triangles.

DISPLAY FRAME

Equipment

- tagboard
- green blotting paper
- corrugated cardboard
- self-adhesive picture hanger
- paste or paper glue
- X-acto knife

Cut out a rectangular piece of tagboard. Cut blotting paper to the same size and paste them together. Make 2 frames of corrugated cardboard, one larger than the other. Paste the first around the blotter and the second, slightly larger, over it. Cut out small cardboard triangles and attach them in a random pattern. Attach the picture hanger to the back.

STORAGE BOXES

Equipment
- 2 cereal boxes, one larger than the other
- corrugated cardboard
- paste
- X-acto knife
- ruler

These handsome storage boxes are nothing more than 2 cereal boxes glued together and covered with corrugated cardboard. Measure the boxes and cut corresponding pieces of cardboard. Put paste on the back side of the cardboard and attach to the boxes. Do not paste the top piece yet.

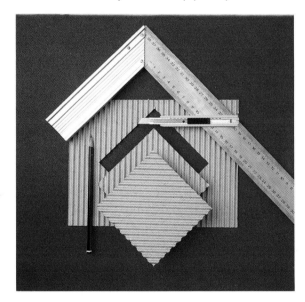

Cut a piece of corrugated cardboard to the size of the top of the storage box. Draw a square in the middle of its back and cut it out with the X-acto knife. Turn the cardboard to the right side. Remove the lozenge, give it a quarter turn, and replace it. The stripes now create an interesting contrast.

COMPACT DISK STORAGE RACK

Equipment
- shoe box
- corrugated cardboard
- paste
- X-acto knife
- ruler

Cut the front of the shoe box at an angle, as shown. Measure, cut, and paste a strip of corrugated cardboard around the box. Add a small triangle of corrugated cardboard on the front.

Any of these cardboard projects can be painted with poster paints or varnished.

The Chinese were not only the first to develop papermaking—they also invented the art of paper cutouts, best represented by their shadow theater. The oldest known book of cutouts in Europe dates to the sixteenth century: the book of the Passion, dedicated to King Henry VII of England.

THE PEARL OF UTRECHT

In the seventeenth century, the city of Utrecht in the Netherlands was known throughout Europe for its paper cutouts. A girl named Anna Maria van Schurman contributed considerably to the fame of the town. By the time she was seven years old, her cutouts were already considered masterpieces. Her portraits of princes and scholars were admired by visitors who visited the city specifically to see them. The pearl of Utrecht, as she was called, did not merely excel in the art of cutouts. She was fluent in five languages, and could write in Arab, Syrian, Ethiopian, and Hebrew. In addition, she was talented in music, drawing, engraving, embroidery, and sculpture!

PAPER HOUSES

In Asia, especially in Japan, paper is used as an architectural element. In traditional rural houses, the floor is often made from a kind of strong paper. Screens, used to create privacy for families living in a single room, are also made of paper. There are even interior walls made from a wood frame and paper. These paper walls allow light to filter throughout the house.

PAPIER-MÂCHÉ

Papier-mâché is made of paper mixed with glue, resin, or another kind of bonding material. The word means "chewed paper," but it can be made of pulp or of sheets of paper glued together. Papier-mâché became popular in Europe in the early eighteenth century, when it was made into trays, boxes, and other small articles, and also into tables and chairs. It can be very strong. During the nineteenth century, a papier-mâché house was built and at one time the Japanese even made armor out of papier-mâché.

SILHOUETTES

Silhouettes were originally portraits in profile, traced from the shadow cast by the subject. They were then cut out of black paper and glued to a white background. They were named after a finance minister, Etienne de Silhouette, who was an extremely unpopular figure in eighteenth-century France, and who made silhouettes as a hobby. The profiles were called silhouettes in reference to the inspector's policies, which left people too poor to afford real portraits—à la Silhouette meant "cheap." Or perhaps the portraits were named after him because he stayed in power only a short time and then disappeared like a shadow.

HANS CHRISTIAN ANDERSEN

Andersen wrote many famous fairy tales, including "The Little Mermaid" and "The Ugly Duckling," but he was also a skilled visual artist who made puppets, drew, and created artwork from cut paper. Andersen made some of his paper cuttings while he was telling his stories.

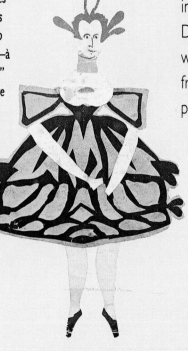

Paper cuttings
by Hans Christian
Andersen.

HANDY DISH

Equipment
- plaster strips
- tube or jar of petroleum jelly
- basin
- scissors

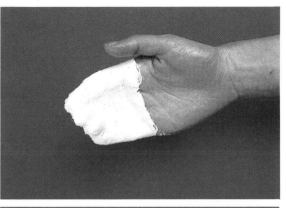

3

1 You'll be able to work with only one hand, so cut at least a dozen short strips of the plaster before starting.
Coat one hand with petroleum jelly. This will make it easier to remove the plaster once it has dried.

2

Plaster strips (plaster of Paris bandages) are available from medical supply stores and art supply stores. Drying time will vary; read the directions on the package.

Place the first strip of plaster in the water and cover your fingertips. Smooth it down well. Keep your fingers together and try not to move.

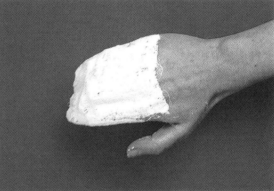

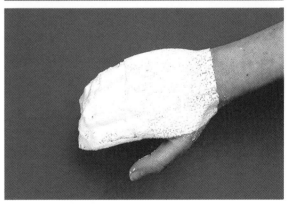

Place 2 strips on the inside of your fingers, covering them completely.
Place 3 strips on the back of your fingers. The strips should cover about half of your hand.
Place 2 strips on the back of your hand. Smooth them down well.

4

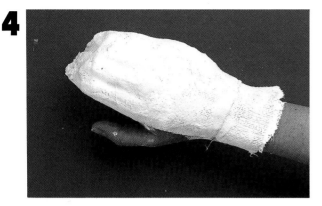

Place 1 strip on the back of your wrist, but don't wrap it all the way around. Let strips dry well and carefully remove this first section.

5

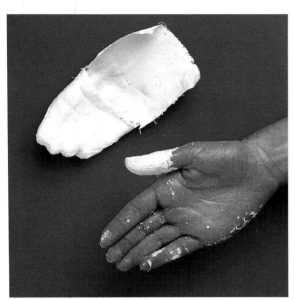

Start the second section by plastering your thumb with a small strip. Smooth it down so it covers your thumb completely. Add a second strip to your thumb.

6

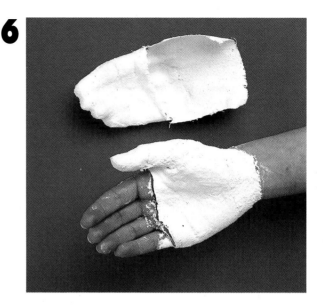

Plaster your palm with several strips. Be sure to keep your palm cupped. Alternate the direction of the strips to add strength.

Place 1 or 2 strips on the inside of your wrist. Let the plaster dry completely and carefully remove this second section.

7

LAMP

Equipment
- adjustable desk lamp
- 2 rolls of plaster strips

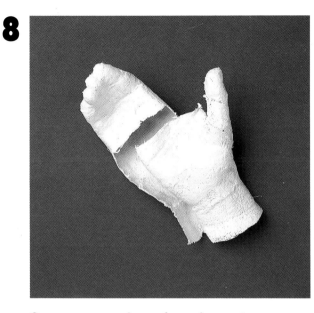

8

Cut any excess plaster from the sections so that they fit together perfectly. To hold them together, add small pieces of plaster strips to the joints. Wrap a large strip all around the wrist. To make dish stronger, stuff paper inside the hand.

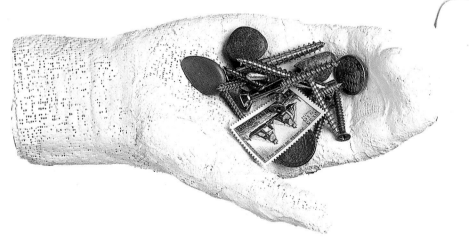

Unplug lamp and remove the light bulb and springs. For the base, place an entire roll of plaster in the water and wind it around the lamp beginning at the bottom. Overlap small strips of plaster to cover the light fixture. Replace the springs and bulb. The lamp will still work, but it will no longer bend.

Clock

Equipment
- wall clock
- 2 rolls of plaster strips
- large piece of thick cardboard
- self-adhesive picture hanger
- pencil
- foam mounting tape
- scissors
- X-acto knife
- ruler

Bookends

Equipment
- 1 roll of plaster strips
- 2 tennis balls
- scissors
- paper tape
- thick cardboard
- X-acto knife

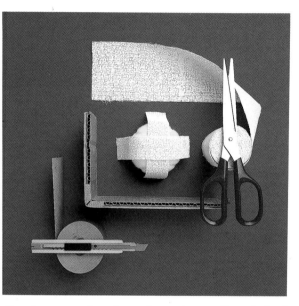

In the middle of a large piece of cardboard, trace the shape of the clock. Measure and cut out the shape of a large cross (or any other shape desired) around the clock. Do not cut the center, where the clock goes. Use scissors to cut large strips of plaster. Dip them in water and crisscross them on the cardboard, leaving the center (where the clock will go) bare. Smooth the strips down and let the plaster dry overnight. Place a few heavy books or other weights on the plastered cardboard so that it doesn't warp.

When the plaster is completely dry, place the clock in the center. Attach the clock to the cardboard with foam mounting tape, making sure it is securely attached. Attach the clock to the wall with a self-adhesive picture hanger.

Cut 4 rectangular pieces from the cardboard, 2 of them longer than the other 2. Connect 1 long and 1 short piece with paper tape, making a square corner. While this dries, cut and moisten narrow strips of plaster and wrap them around the tennis balls. Crisscross the bands around the balls and let them dry. When the paper tape is dry, dip the remaining plaster strips in water and wind them around the bookends.

Moisten the tennis balls; they will stick easily to the bookends.

CASTING

Plaster is the best material for making casts. The Greeks used the technique of casting to make many of their statues. The sculptor made a clay model and coated it with animal fat. Then several layers of plaster were applied to the statue. Carefully removing the plaster from the clay created a hollow mo which the molten t was poured. Whe bronze cooled hardened, the pl: was removed.

Statue of the French writer Balzac, by Auguste Rodin, 1897.

MUMMIES

Egyptians mummified the bodies of their dead to preserve them. They prepared the body by removing the brain and other internal organs (except for the heart and kidneys). The inside of the body was filled with resin or sawdust and then the openings were sewed shut. After the body was dried, it was wrapped with strips of fabric. The mummy's mouth was left open so that the soul was free to come and go. Sometimes the mummy's face was covered with a mask. The Egyptians mummified the bodies of kings, queens, priests, and priestesses. They also mummified animals that were sacred to the gods: cats, bulls, and ibises (a kind of bird).

Egyptian art, 31st dynasty (about 340 B.C.). Mummy and coffin of a priestess.

MASKS

Every civilization throughout history, from the Greeks to the Egyptians, from the Africans to the Inuit, from the Japanese to the Indians, have made masks.

In Greek theater, the actors wore masks that were intended to reveal an emotion or a trait of the character they were playing. Sometimes the mask had two sides and the actor would turn around to reveal another aspect of the character. The masks generally fell into three categories: tragic, comic, or satirical.

In Japan, the mask is an essential element of No theater. No is a dramatic genre that consists of a long poem that is sung, danced, and mimed. Created in the fifteenth century, this theater is still popular today. No theater uses many different kinds of masks, of five general types: old people (male and female), gods, goddesses, devils, and goblins. The masks are made of wood coated with plaster and then lacquered. The different colors of the masks have traditional meanings. For instance, white is the color of a corrupt ruler and red is the color of a righteous man.

Japanese art.
No mask.

The contemporary artist Christo began wrapping the Pont Neuf in Paris on September 23, 1985. The bridge stayed wrapped in 4000 square meters of fabric for 15 days.

The Commedia dell'arte represented an important step in the history of Italian theater, because it inspired many theatrical genres, including vaudeville and comic opera. Commedia dell'arte was a street theater; companies of actors traveled from town to town, playing at fairs and in marketplaces. The actors were excellent mimes and generally used masks to identify the ten central characters that appeared in all the plays.

GALAXY STENCILS

Equipment
- 3 picture frames (all the same size)
- tagboard
- Bristol board
- off-white drawing paper
- large potato
- 3 self-adhesive picture hangers
- stencil or poster paints (red, blue, yellow, and gold)
- stencil brush
- drawing compass
- pencil
- small knife
- scissors
- ruler

2

Draw a comet on one of sheets of Bristol board and cut it out with the X-acto knife. Then use the drawing compass to draw Saturn on another piece of Bristol board. Cut it out.

Follow these directions to learn how to make stencils, then create new designs.

1

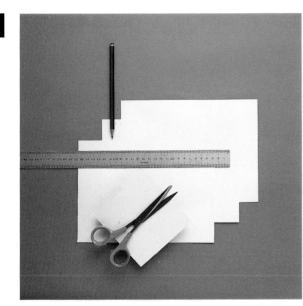

Measure and cut 3 sheets of drawing paper to the dimensions of the frames, 3 sheets of tagboard (for the back of the frames), and 2 sheets of Bristol board (for the stencils).

3

Place the comet stencil on the drawing paper. Dip the brush in the red paint and start to dab in the head of the comet.

4 Without moving the stencil, color in the yellow in the same way, so that the colors mix gradually. The paint dries fairly quickly. Place the decorated sheet of paper on the tagboard, then place a piece of glass on the front and frame the stencil. Attach the picture hanger to the back and hang it on the wall.

5

Place the Saturn stencil on a sheet of drawing paper. Dip the brush in the blue paint and dab all around the stencil and in the cutout areas. It's possible to get different shades by dabbing different amounts of paint in selected areas. Frame the stencil as instructed for the comet.

6

Making potato stamps is easy and fun. Draw small stars on a piece of Bristol board. Cut them out using an X-acto knife. Cut the potato in half, place the stars on one side, and cut away the potato, leaving several stars shapes in relief (sticking up). Cut more stars in the other side of the potato.

7

Dip the brush in the gold paint, then in the yellow paint. Dab the paint onto the stars on the potato, then press the potato on the drawing paper. Repeat several times, putting more paint on the potato each time.

When it is completely dry, frame the stars as instructed for the comet. The gold paint will make the stars shine.

WINDOW SHADE

To decorate a window shade, make several stencils by drawing Jupiter, the Moon, stars, and Saturn on sheets of Bristol board. See photograph for suggestions. Place the stencils all around the shade and apply the paint, mixing several colors. Add other planets or even the Big Dipper.

CHAIR

Remove the cloth back from a director's chair. Dab paint on the soles of a pair of shoes and "walk" them (with your hands) across the fabric. Reapply paint to the shoes after each print.

TRUNK

To make a star-studded trunk, use a stencil with lots of small stars. Pick a color of paint that contrasts with the color of the trunk.

Other stencil and stamp ideas: 1. Cut patterns from apples to use as stamps. 2. Dip small flat toys in paint and print them on a T-shirt. 3. Use stencils to make table mats or decorate the walls of your room.

PRINTING ON CLOTH

The Chinese invented printing. They used engraved wooden blocks that were coated with a color and pressed onto paper or fabric. This produced a printed design that corresponded to the shape of the block. Around the seventeenth century, traders returned to Europe from India with waterfast and fade-resistant cotton fabrics, printed with iridescent colors. European silk and wool weavers quickly imitated these new fabrics.

PRINTING IN INDIA: A NOBLE ART

In India, printing on cloth is still done by hand. Printers use wooden blocks to create designs. The outside surface of the block is carved, then it is dipped in paint and pressed onto the fabric. The operation is repeated over the entire surface to be printed. A separate block is used for each color of dye.

Dyers, as well as printers, are highly respected artisans. They have learned to make indelible dyes by developing chemical painting and dyeing techniques that modify the structure of the fiber itself.

BATIK

Batik means "wax painting." Using this technique, which also originated in China, a wax drawing is made on fabric. Wherever the wax has been painted, the dye does not color the fabric. The dyer can dip the cloth more than once to blend colors, or boil off the old wax and apply new. The technique is often used to decorate Indian cottons.

Wood block for fabric printing. India. State of Rajasthan.

Right: Detail of a batik. Sri Lanka.

Below: Cotton fabric created by Fernand Léger in 1956. Printed in the United States.

Upper right: Toile de Jouy. Seventeenth century.

STENCILS

Stencils are an ancient means of decorating a surface. The Egyptians used stencils in 2500 B.C., and the Inuit people cut stencils from sealskin long before their culture encountered Western civilization.

Stencils were popular in the United States during the nineteenth century. Unable to afford expensive imported wall coverings of paper or fabric, people stenciled designs on their walls. Families could decorate their own walls or hire traveling artists to do it for them. Designs were also stenciled onto furniture.

The first factory for printing fabrics was built in Jouy, France, in 1760. Originally the designs were printed from wood blocks, but after 1770 copper plates were used as well. The beautiful fabrics created there were known throughout the world. Even today, toile de Jouy (fabric of Jouy) is the name used to refer to cotton cloth printed with designs of landscapes and figures.

INDEX

First American edition 1994 published by Ticknor & Fields Books for Young Readers, A Houghton Mifflin company, 215 Park Avenue South, New York, New York 10003. • Copyright © by Hachette, Paris, 1992 • English translation copyright © 1994 by Ticknor & Fields Books for Young Readers • First published in France by Hachette • All rights reserved. • For information about permission to reproduce selections from this book, write to Permissions, Ticknor & Fields, 215 Park Avenue South, New York, New York 10003. • Manufactured in France • The text of this book is set in 13 point Gill Sans

10 9 8 7 6 5 4 3 2 1

Photo credits: © Adagp / musée national d'Art moderne, page 15 • © Jean-Loup Charmet, pages 22, 23 • © Didier Dorval / Explorer, page 55 • © Edimedia, pages 46, 55 • © Gamma, pages 22, 31 • © Giraudon, page 46 • © Harry Gruyaert / Magnum, page 47 • © de Keerle-Spooner / Gamma, page 31 • © Kharbine / Tapabor, page 39 • © Lauros Giraudon, page 47 • © J. A. Lavaud / Artephot, page 55 • © News / Gamma, page 31 • © Parker-Spooner / Gamma, page 30 • © Photothèque du musée de l'Homme, page 54 • © Spadem / musée national d'Art moderne, page 54 • © Léonard de Selva, page 14 • © de Selva / Tapabor, page 38 • © Snark / Edimedia, page 39

Library of Congress Cataloging-in-Publication Data

Guerrier, Charlie.
   A collage of crafts / by Charlie Guerrier; photographs by Marc Schwartz; research by Etienne Colomb. — 1st American ed.
     p. cm. — (Young artisan)
   Includes index.
   Summary: Basic crafts using common objects such as leaves, shells, newspaper, cardboard, and stencils.
   ISBN 0-395-68377-7
   1. Handicraft—Juvenile literature. 2. Decoration and ornament—Juvenile literature. [1. Handicraft.] I. Schwartz, Marc, ill. II. Title. III. Series.
TT160.G9213 1994
745.5—dc20   93-24968   CIP   AC

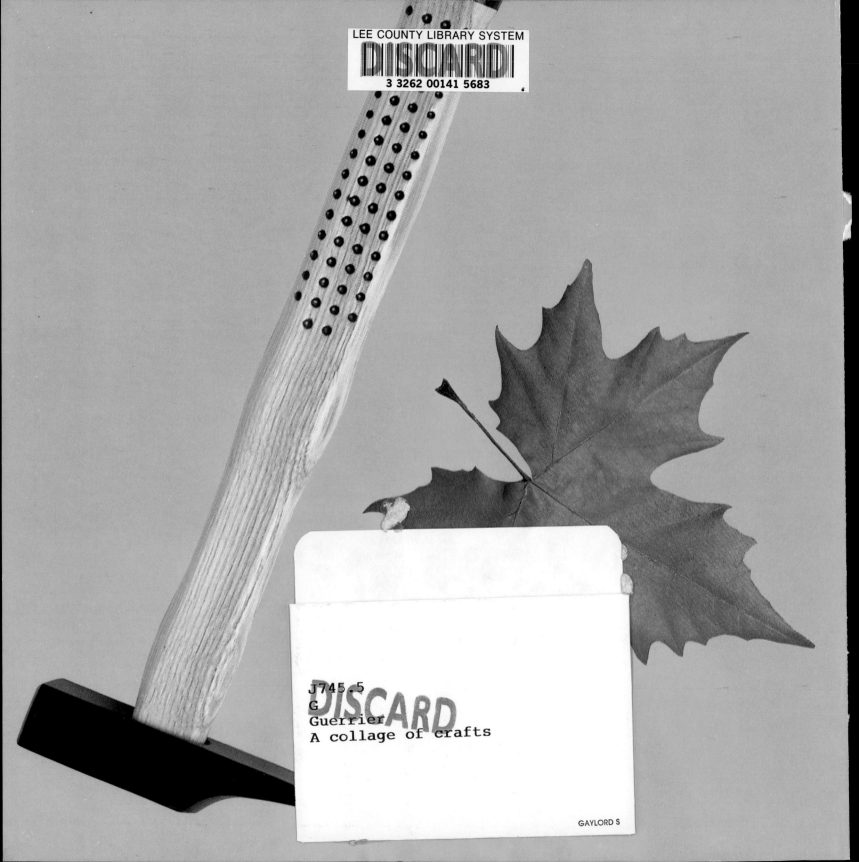